LONDON MIDLAND STEAM IN ACTION 2

W. A. Blake

D. BRADFORD BARTON LIMITED

Frontispiece: Stanier Class 5 No. 44804, from Saltley shed at Birmingham, about to come off the southbound 'Devonian' at Bristol (Temple Meads) on 26 September 1958. This inter-Regional express, from Bradford (Forster Square) to Paignton, will be worked on from this point by a Western Region 'Castle'.   [J. R. Besley]

© copyright D. Bradford Barton Ltd 1975   ISBN 0 85153 164 4

printed in Great Britain by Chapel River Press (IPC Printers), Andover

for the publishers

D. BRADFORD BARTON LTD · Trethellan House · Truro · Cornwall · England

introduction

The L.M.S., serving the Midlands, the industrial north-west and Scotland, as well as providing the principal link with Ireland, was the richest and most powerful of the pre-Nationalisation companies. At Nationalisation, its dominance became apparent and for something like a decade the L.M.S. look changed surprisingly little on what had become the London Midland Region of British Railways. On other Regions, the effect was more marked, not least by the introduction of B.R. Standard classes of locomotives which were, in effect, up-dated designs of obvious L.M.S. parentage. That the honour of being the last stronghold of steam on Britain's main lines fell to the L.M. Region was not surprising—a reflection of its dominance and its well-ordered range of relatively up-to-date motive power that had been inherited from the L.M.S.R. in 1948, twenty years before. Thus the illustrations in this volume, although all taken in post-Nationalisation years, could well be of the old L.M.S.R., except in a few details. Not surprisingly, steam on these former lines has a following among enthusiasts that is only exceeded by that of the former Great Western, where fierce loyalties are proverbial. It is hoped that these pages portray something of the character of the L.M.S.; we all have our favourite memories, all of which are, alas, now fading with the passage of time—perhaps a 'Jubilee', behind time and being worked to the limit, on the climb to Ais Gill; an ageing Class 2P 4-4-0 working out her time on three-coach locals out of Bedford; a 'Duchess'—finest of them all—sweeping down Madeley bank with 'The Royal Scot'; or the sight and sound of an 8F 2-8-0 slogging up to Standedge tunnel with a heavy load of Yorkshire coal. Even the Class Fives, ten years ago so commonplace they were barely given a second glance, would now be a noble sight heading a rake of well-worn stock on one of the once innumerable summer excursions to Blackpool or Llandudno. Memories remain, too, of the sounds as well as the sights, ranging from the quick three-cylinder exhaust beat of a rebuilt 'Royal Scot' at speed, the wheezy 1/2/3/4 rhythm of a G2 0-8-0 goods from L.N.W.R. days, or the clank of rods on an elderly 'Patriot'. Alas, except at a few places such as Dinting, Carnforth and Tyseley, L.M. steam is now gone, replaced on the West Coast main line by faceless electrics and elsewhere by anonymous diesels.

'The Ulster Express' constituted the principal LMS service to Northern Ireland, running between Euston and Heysham, connecting with steamers plying to Belfast. Inaugurated in 1927, it was invariably a 'Royal Scot' or, later, a Pacific turn. No. 46244 *King George VI*, of Camden shed, rests by the buffer stops at Euston after bringing the express in, 30 July 1957.

[A. R. Butcher]

No. 46203 *Princess Margaret Rose* backing out of Euston, 12 April 1957. These first Stanie Pacifics had a long, lean look compared to the later 'Duchesses'—partly due to the not being fitted with smoke deflectors. The smaller diameter boiler of the earlier clas did not necessitate these.

[A. R. Butche

Morning arrivals at Euston, 10 May 1958; 'Britannia' Class Pacific No. 70045 *Lord Rowallan* with the 1.10 a.m. from Holyhead at Platform No. 1 and No. 46257 *City of Salford* with the 10.20 p.m. ex-Glasgow. Note the wheel retarders in front of the buffer stops. [R. K. Taylor]

In the spring of 1955, one of the later Stanier Pacifics, No. 46237 *City of Bristol*, was transferred to Western Region for a series of trials on expresses to Bristol and the West of England. Crewed by Old Oak Common men, she worked 'The Cornish Riviera' to Plymouth on more than one occasion, and with conspicuous success. Here, No. 46237 has arrived at Paddington with an express from Birkenhead, 26 April 1955.
[R. K. Taylor]

During January and February 1956, Stanier Pacifics were again seen working out of Paddington, supplying motive power for various of the principal WR expresses at a time when the 'King' Class 4-6-0s had been temporarily withdrawn due to bogie defects. 'Princess Royal' Class No. 46210 *Lady Patricia* adds a graceful touch to the Paddington scene, on the 10.30 a.m. for Penzance, 10 February 1956.
[R. K. Taylor]

Adorned with the handsome 'Caledonian' headboard, No. 46239 *City of Chester* comes up Camden bank in the usual effortless Stanier Pacific style, surefooted and with steam to spare. This express was the successor to the pre-war 'Coronation Scot', between Euston and Glasgow Central.   [A. R. Butcher]

Rebuilt 'Royal Scot' No. 46119 *Lancashire Fusilier* steams through Bushey and Oxhey on an up express, with sixteen miles more to go to Euston. No. 46119, allocated to Crewe North, was rebuilt in 1944 and withdrawn in 1963. In August 1950 she was involved in a collision at Penmaenmawr when heading the up 'Irish Mail'. At 3 a.m., with sixteen on, and doing almost seventy, she collided with a 2-6-0 running light, six persons being killed and many injured. Although seriously damaged, No. 46119 was rebuilt and back in service in 1951.   [A. R. Butcher]

'Jubilee' Class No. 45737 *Atlas* going well through Watford Junction with an up Birmingham express, 12 April 1957.   [A. R. Butcher]

12

The fireman of ex-LNWR G2 No. 48952 keeps a sharp look-out from the footplate on a curve near Watford, on a southbound freight bound for Willesden, 2 June 1956. In appearance as well as in sound, no one was likely to confuse a G2 with any other 0-8-0.

[A. R. Butcher]

An up relief express from Blackpool leaves Watford Tunnel behind No. 46168 *The Girl Guide*. She was the next to the last to be built of the 'Royal Scots', turned out from Derby in 1930.

[S. Creer]

scene in the cutting
orth of Watford
unnels, with No. 46211
ueen Maud on a
verpool-bound
xpress. The up and
wn fast and slow
es diverge here to
ss through separate
res.   [A. R. Butcher]

Rebuilt 'Patriot'
No. 45735 *Comet* on a
fast freight north of
Bletchley. She was
rebuilt with a larger
boiler and double
chimney in 1942 and
subsequently
re-classified 7P, as
with the rebuilt
Scots'.   [L. Waters]

Old and new on West Coast main line freights; above, G2a 0-8-0 No.49157, dating back to the Bowen-Cooke era, and Class 8F 2-8-0 No. 48733, built in the Second World War under LNER auspices. It was a reflection of the undemanding nature of freight working on the Western Division south of Crewe that such disparate designs were still regularly seen side by side as late as 1951.

[B. A. Butt]

Class 3F 0-6-0T No.47500 shunting at Bletchley. These handy LMS tanks, introduced from 1924 onwards, eventually numbered over 400 and were familiar everywhere on the system. Quite why the name 'Jinty' came to be given to this class by enthusiasts is not clear, for this was never a railwayman's nickname for them.

[L. Waters]

A close-up of No.46114 *Coldstream Guardsman*, from Edge Hill shed (8a), awaiting the 'right-away' at Rugby, on 23 July 1959, with the up 'Manxman' (2 p.m. Liverpool–Euston). The inset curved smoke deflectors of the rebuilt 'Scots' was a distinctive feature viewed from a forward angle.   [M. J. Jackson]

An interesting assortment of coaching stock makes up the load for Class 5 No.45449 from Springs Branch shed, seen easing slowly past Rugby station.   [M. J. Jackson

No.46118 *Royal Welsh Fusilier* entering Rugby with the 8.10 a.m. Llandudno to Euston July 1959. She had run over 2 million miles upon withdrawal in 1964.   [M. J. Jackson

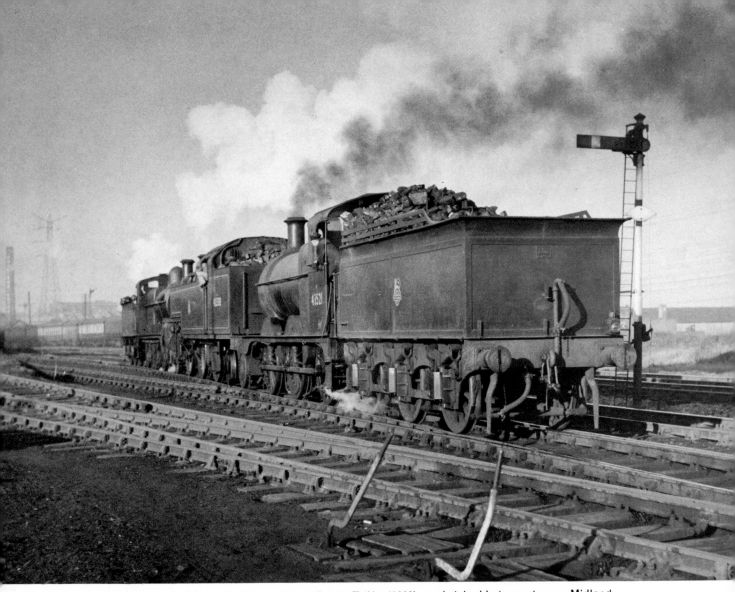

An interesting trio, consisting of a Fowler Class 4P 2-6-4T (No. 42338) sandwiched between two ex-Midland 3F 0-6-0s, coming off shed at Bourneville (21B) near Birmingham. [A. R. Butcher]

New Street, Birmingham: above, one of the ubiquitous Class Fives, No. 45231, about to leave with the 3.45 p.m. to Liverpool (Lime Street), 28 April 1959 [R. K. Taylor] and (below) No. 46167 *The Hertfordshire Regiment* making something of a fuss at the start of a run to Euston, 6 February 1958. The latter engine is in green, a livery that always looked alien on ex-LMSR classes. [A. R. Butcher]

Another of the good-looking 'Jubilees', No. 45725 *Repulse*, at Gloucester. As a class they were overshadowed by the all-round brilliance of the smaller Class 5s—which were well-nigh their equal—and the success of the rebuilt 'Scots', which were vastly stronger.

[M. J. Jackson]

ubilee' No. 45700 *Amethyst* at Kings Norton on 10 May 1963. Having brought an overnight fitted freight to the sidings, she is backing down into the sunrise on the direct line to Saltley shed. Originally No. 45700 as named *Britannia* but was re-christened in 1951 to commemorate the frigate involved in the Yangtse cident of 1949, and also to enable the former name to be transferred to the first of the new BR Standard acifics.

[P. J. Shoesmith]

A grey February day in 1957 on Lickey, and 'Jubilee' Class No. 45685 *Barfleur* has wet rails to contend with on the 1 in 37. Helping mightily in the rear with this Bristol–York express is Standard 9F No. 92079—at this date the principal banker on the incline.

[A. R. Butcher]

Another 'Jubilee' on Lickey, coming up the gradient with a north-bound express on a winter day in 1958. No. 45660 *Rooke* was one of the 'Admirals' series in the class.

[A. R. Butcher]

A scene at Bromsgrove on 16 April 1955, with the well known ex-MR 0-10-0 No.58100 gingerly buffering up to the 'beaver-tail' observation car at the rear of an excursion bound for Birmingham (New Street). This locomotive, a four-cylinder 'one-off' built at Derby immediately after the First World War specifically for duty on Lickey, was retired in May 1956 and condemned at Derby works a few weeks later.

[R. K. Taylor]

Full of age and anachronism—ex-M R Class 2F 0-6-0 No. 58286 at Birmingham (New Street). Although it is April 1955, she still has L M S initials on the tender, and it is longer still since such a veteran ever had the chance to lay claim to correct use of an express passenger headlamp code . . .

[R. K. Taylor]

Lower quadrant signals betray the 'foreign' setting for No. 46157 *The Royal Artilleryman*, photographed at Oxford on 23 May 1962. She is backing through from the shed to Hinksey Yard to work a freight north to Birmingham. The 'Royal Scots' were all but new locomotives, so extensive and radical was their 're-build' at the time. [J. R. Besley]

Fowler 2-6-4T No. 42327 leaving Studley with an Ashchurch–Birmingham local, 4 April 1959. This line via Evesham and Redditch has long been closed and the track removed, except the Redditch–Birmingham section.

[P. J. Shoesmith]

Stanier Class 5 No. 44966, from Saltley shed, at Worcester (Shrub Hill). She is working the 1.45 p.m. ex-Gloucester and is collecting two more coaches before departing at 2.50 p.m. for New Street, Birmingham; 25 May 1962.

[J. R. Besley]

H. G. Ivatt-designed
2-6-2T No. 41226 heads
a push–pull two-coach
train near Southam &
Long Itchington on
3 August 1956. One of
the cement works
typical of this part of
Warwickshire is
prominent in the
background.

[P. J. Shoesmith]

The fine lines of one of Stanier's 'Jubilees' is seen to advantage in this overhead view of No. 45686 *St. Vincent* at the north end of Crewe station, heading a troop train south, June 1957.   [S. D. Wainwright]

Another of the 'Jubilees' named in honour of a naval battle, No.45681 *Aboukir* drifts into Crewe off the Chester line on 26 June 1957. In the foreground is Class 2P No.40659, one of the LMS versions of the earlier Midland design of 4-4-0. With 6ft 9in coupled wheels (7ft in the case of the MR ones) these were real 'high-steppers'—useful for decorative piloting or smart work with an inspection saloon, but sadly lacking in tractive effort for stop-and-start local passenger use. [R. H. Short]

Rebuilt 'Royal Scot' No. 46109 *Royal Engineer* leaving Crewe for Euston, 4 July 1959. She was one of the first of the class to be rebuilt with larger boiler, double chimney and other modifications (in 1943) and ran without smoke deflectors until after Nationalisation. [T. Lewis; N. E. Preedy collection]

The 3F tanks, so commonplace in yards and stations throughout LM Region, seemed surprisingly rare on the open road. Here No.47371 canters along at Chester, heading a short freight for the sidings at Mold Junction, 8 May 1961. It is just crossing a bridge carrying the GW and LMS metals over the Shropshire Union Canal. [P. H. Hanson]

Looking decidedly alien as a result of losing the top rim of her chimney casting, Hughes Mogul No. 42827 leaves Chester with a train for Birkenhead in July 1962. The ex-LNWR signal gantry here, at the west end of the station, was a well known feature for many years.

[E. N. Kneale]

After a stop at Chester, No. 46233 *Duchess of Sutherland* gets into her stride again with a Euston–Holyhead express, in March 1963. The North Wales expresses were once the sole preserve of the 'Royal Scots' but 'Duchesses' helped out towards the end of steam when the introduction of Class 40 diesels meant they were no longer vital on the faster Anglo-Scottish services.   [J. R. Carter]

Coupled to a self-weighing tender, on extended trials, Class 5 No. 44986 heads into Chester through one of the sandstone cuttings just west of the station. She is bound from her home shed at Mold Junction to Warrington with coal empties. [J. R. Carter]

No. 46248 *City of Leeds* near Chester getting under way again after a signal check with 'The Irish Mail'. The normal—and fitting—maroon livery of these 'Duchess' class Pacifics was restored from 1958 onwards, after a decade of non-LMSR colours.

[J. R. Carter]

Once the compounds and the surviving ex-LNWR types had gone from the North Wales coast line, the standard locomotive class on all passenger services, except through expresses and locals, was the 'Black Five'. On summer Saturdays, in the immediate post-war years, they headed train after train, running almost block and block even on the quadruple track through Rhyl and Prestatyn, and bunching up where there was only one double track between Llandulas and Colwyn Bay. Here, No. 45243 is approaching the latter station with a train from Manchester, in the summer of 1962. [E. N. Kneale]

A close-up of well-kept No. 46148 *The Manchester Regiment* at Llandudno Junction in May 1964, with her crew awaiting the right-away for Bangor and Holyhead. A short sharp climb punctuating this largely sea-level route faces trains going westward immediately after leaving the station, at about 1 in 100 up to the portal of the tubular bridge over the river Conway.
[E. N. Kneale]

The 6H shed plate on No. 42579 marks her as being from Bangor, where a fair number of Stanier two-cylinder 2-6-4 tanks were allocated to handle local trains on the Holyhead–Llandudno Junction section. The setting is Menai Bridge station, closed in 1966, where the Caernarvon and Afonwen branch left the main line to Holyhead. The bridge lies about a mile away.
[M. J. Jackson]

Another of the Stanier
2-6-4 tanks from Bangor
shed, No. 42608, about to
add its quota of smoke to
the already murky tunnel
outside the station, heading
a Butlin's Special to the
holiday camp at Pwllheli in
the summer of 1963. Bangor
station lies in a confined
situation between two
tunnels and shunting
operations at each end of
the station frequently
entailed movements within
these.   [E. N. Kneale]

A view along the flanks of
No. 46228 *Duchess of Rutland*
on shed at Holyhead on a
Sunday in July 1960.
           [E. N. Kneale]

'Patriot' Class 6P No. 45546 *Fleetwood* at speed with a Euston-bound cup-tie special passing through the former station at Minshull Vernon, five miles or so north of Crewe on the main line, 29 April 1959. No. 45546 a few years earlier was involved in a collision in fog near Crewe while working a fitted freight and overturned, killing the driver. Although damage was serious, she was repaired and returned to traffic, being finally withdrawn in 1962 along with numerous other of these so-called 'Baby Scots'. [P. H. Hanson]

Heading a morning Liverpool (Lime Street) to Birmingham (New Street) express, 'Jubilee' No. 45554 *Quebec* passes Winsford Junction in Cheshire on an April day in 1959. Her external condition is no credit to the cleaners at Edge Hill shed.   [P. H. Hanson]

Class 5 No. 45410 hurries an eleven-coach Liverpool–Birmingham express through now demolished Sefton Park station on the outskirts of Liverpool. On the down fast line, an 8F can be seen backing down to Edge Hill shed. [P. H. Hanson]

One of the Edge Hill 'Royal Scots', No. 46156 *The South Wales Borderer*, comes over the bridge at Runcorn crossing the Mersey with the up 'Merseyside Express' on a misty morning in May 1959. [P. H. Hanson]

The 7.00 p.m. to Leeds City a few minutes before departure from Liverpool (Lime Street) in December 1956.
[R. K. Taylor]

In ex-works condition, No. 46234 *Duchess of Abercorn* (from 12b, Carlisle Upperby), passing through Edge Hill station on the initial steep climb out of Lime Street with an express for the West of England, 17 April 1960. She will work through as far as Shrewsbury.

[P. H. Hanson]

The driver of 'Princess Royal' Class No. 46211 *Queen Maud* keeps a watchful eye on the road ahead as he brings the 10.05 a.m. (Sunday) Lime Street–Euston up past Edge Hill depot on 16 August 1959. These earlier Stanier Pacifics were regulars on the Liverpool services throughout their career.   [P. H. Hanson]

Edge Hill station again, and No. 46110 *Grenadier Guardsman* coming out of one of the many short tunnels up from Lime Street, at the head of a West of England express bound for Plymouth.　　[P. H. Hanson]

Manchester Central, with Class 4P Fairburn 2-6-4T No. 42113 on the 10.30 a.m. for Sheffield, 15 March 1963. On the left, the tender of Class 4F 2-6-0 No. 43036 is visible.　　[J. R. Besley]

Second to be built of the 'Jubilees', No. 45553 *Canada* heads a Blackpool express out of Manchester Exchange. She was one of 64 in the class withdrawn in 1964, in the case of No. 45553 after thirty years of service.

[J. R. Carter]

A Stockport local near London Road station in Manchester behind Fowler 4P 2-6-4T No. 42309, 30 August 1952. The LMS put 125 of these tanks into service for short distance passenger work; they were built in two types which differed only in the size of the cab.

[T. Lewis; N. E. Preedy collection]

Drifting down the 1 in 104 of Boars Head bank ready for the stop at Wigan (North Western), No. 45542 has charge of a Workington and Barrow–Euston express, 23 April 1960. She was one of the un-named 'Patriots', a class with no common theme to its series of names. The 'Baby Scots' were well liked by footplatemen and compared more than favourably with their 'Jubilee' rivals.

[P. H. Hanson]

In the early 1960's, LM Region introduced a new headboard for the principal Anglo-Scottish daytime express, utilising a tartan background for the name 'Royal Scot' and with a lion above this as an emblem. No. 46229 *Duchess of Hamilton* displays this as the express passes Boars Head Junction north of Wigan, 1 May 1954. Less noticeable from this low angle is the tapered top to the smokebox—a legacy from the days when this was one of the 'Coronation' streamliners. A further final touch to the Royal Scot about this time was a similar nameboard at the tail end of the last coach, mounted on the corridor connection.

[T. Lewis; N. E. Preedy collection]

A cheerful wave from the fireman to the photographer on the platform of deserted Milnthorpe station as No. 45599 *Bechuanaland* speeds through, 10 September 1956. This is at the southern end of the climb over Shap, from near sea level at Carnforth up over the summit and so to the flat coastal plain at Carlisle.

[T. Lewis; N. E. Preedy collection]

Class 5 No. 45431 with a returning Heysham–Manchester excursion passing over Brock water troughs north of Preston, May 1956. [T. Lewis; N. E. Preedy collection]

Exceptionally, Stanier 8Fs were occasionally seen in summer pressed into service on excursions or other specials but their use in this capacity was officially frowned upon. No. 48275 is seen on a three-coach local for Wigan on the main line near Leyland on a summer evening in 1965. [K. R. Pirt]

A wet day—alas, far from untypical—at Windermere (Lakeside) terminus
with 'Jubilee' No. 45641 *Sandwich*, from Nottingham shed, about to
depart.   [L. Waters]

One of the Class 4F Moguls introduced by H. G. Ivatt shortly before Nationalisation of the LMS, No. 43008 was a forerunner of a similar BR Standard class later. The high-set running plate, exposed piping, and general angularity made for cheaper costs of manufacture and maintenance, but not for looks—although some of the class were fitted with double chimneys which balanced their lines.   [M. J. Jackson]

Class 5 No. 45019, at the head of a fitted freight, taking water on Tebay troughs, June 1963.

[J. R. Carter]

With only nine coaches on, No. 46229 *Duchess of Hamilton* has no need of a banker and comes confidentl͏ up the 1 in 75 with the northbound Royal Scot, *sans* headboard, on 8 September 1960. Even on wet rail after a shower of rain, she is as sure-footed as any Pacific can be expected to be and, as always with th͏ 'Duchesses', has ample steam to spare.

[A. R. Butcher]

Another of the LMS stalwarts—albeit a smaller one, on Shap; Horwich Mogul No. 42940 quietly masterin͏ the climb near Scout Green with a train of milk tanks and parcel vans for Carlisle on the same date.

[A. R. Butcher]

No. 46201 *Princess Elizabeth* gives another demonstration of the ability of the Stanier Pacifics—lifting a well filled fourteen coach Birmingham–Glasgow express up the last mile or so to Shap summit on 6 July 1958. Incredible loads were worked by these magnificent Pacifics over Shap and Beattock in wartime— often with sixteen and seventeen bogies on, heavily laden with service personnel, without bankers or pilots.

[R. H. Leslie]

One of the Carlisle (Kingmoor) 8Fs, No. 48426, raises a smoke pall at Penrith getting under way again with a train of empty banana vans after a stop for water on 27 July 1963. She has one of the narrower ex-MR tenders, having exchanged her original Stanier high sided type with a 'Jubilee'.

[R. H. Leslie]

A superb study of No. 46256 *Sir William A. Stanier F.R.S.*, recovering speed from a signal check, on the curve at Eamont Junction, with a Glasgow–Euston express, 1 September 1957. One of the last pair of the 'Coronation Pacifics', built in 1947–8, and modified in detail by H. G. Ivatt, No. 46256 could lay claim to be the finest express passenger locomotive Britain has ever seen.
[R. H. Leslie]

The Ivatt Moguls were endearing little machines and for years graced the branch from the main line at Penrith to Keswick and beyond. No. 46491, in admirable condition, leaves the former station with the Keswick and Workington portions of 'The Lakes Express' from Euston, on the same day. This was one of the LMS expresses with a headboard only rarely seen, due to the complexities of the locomotive workings involved.
[R. H. Leslie]

No. 46222 *Queen Mary*, from Polmadie shed, raises an impressive cloud of smoke on th
1 in 131 climb south from Carlisle towards Wreay with a Birmingham-bound expres
25 November 1963.

[R. H. Lesli

The heavy Crewe–Carlisle parcels trains were demanding turns that seldom saw any-
thing less than a 'Duchess' or a pair of smaller locomotives. On a July day in 1958, however,
'Patriot' Class No. 45513 heads gamely north towards Penrith unaided, despite a for-
bidding load of bogie vans and four-wheelers.

[R. H. Leslie]

Another of the Coronation Pacifics at Carlisle (Citadel)—No. 46252 *City of Leicester* waiting to leave for Perth on 7 August 1961. From Kingmoor shed, she has just taken over from a Crewe (South) member of the same class and is seen in the green livery which in the later years of service distinguished the Scottish-based Stanier Pacifics after the majority had reverted to their original maroon. [P. H. Hanson]

In a setting not quite as rural as at first it seems, Ivatt 2-6-0 No. 46426 shuttles from Upperby carriage sidings to Carlisle (Citadel) with empty stock. [M. Dunnett]

8F No. 48438, with an up freight, about to replenish her water supply at Appleby, on the Settle & Carlisle section, July 1965. She was Swindon built, in the early war years. This photograph shows the Type 2 all-welded 4,000 gallon Stanier tender, with 9 ton coal capacity and 53 ton 16 cwt all-up weight.   [K. R. Pirt]

Amid typical 'Dales' scenery in the limestone uplands of West Yorkshire, a Horwich Mogul near Long Preston with an eight-coach Leeds–Morecambe train. At Settle Junction it will leave the main line, to take the 'Little North-Western' line for Carnforth.

[M. Dunnett]

A familiar face beneath the overbridge at derelict Gisburn station, on the Blackburn–Hellifield line—Class 8F 2-8-0 No. 48421, 29 April 1967. This particular member of the class was Swindon built, in 1943, and came back into LMS stock just before Nationalisation. [R. H. Short]

A close-up of Horwich-built Mogul No.42706 waiting to leave Colne station on 15 June 1957 with the 3.35 p.m. to Stockport. At this date she was one of three based upon Rosegrove shed at Burnley, many of the class being allocated to east Lancashire for passenger work. Their massive appearance belied what was really quite a modest size, being a smaller version of the husky Hughes L & Y 4-6-0s. These Moguls also had something of the same stentorian exhaust blast of the former, which were real heavyweights in both sound and appearance.

[R. H. Short]

One of a dozen or more preserved 'Black Fives' is No. 44806, now preserved by the Lakeside & Haverthwaite Railway Co Ltd and is well known in action on their line to Lake Windermere. She is seen here at Colne with a parcels train on an evening in June 1968.

[R. H. Short]

No. 45076 was one of the earlier Class 5s, built by Vulcan Foundry in 1935 with domeless boiler; she is seen here with another of the class doubleheading the heavy Redbridge parcels out of York in July 1965.

[K. R. Pirt]

Stanier 8F No. 48006 from Kirkby shed, at Heaton Mersey, near Stockport, with a down goods, 29 May 1952. She is seen in original condition, with the domeless taper boiler which marked the first twelve 8Fs produced at Crewe in 1935. This was the heavy freight workhorse on the LMS and LM Region, highly regarded by footplate crews and operating staff in every respect.   [T. Lewis; N. E. Preedy collection]

Stanier Mogul No. 42960 heading south near Jodrell Bank with a London Road–Crewe parcels train, 12 April 1958. Posts are in position as evidence of impending electrification. This interesting class of locomotive—one of which is fortunately due for preservation— represented a midway Swindon-cum-Horwich design compromise in Sir William Stanier's early years as CME.   [T. Lewis; N. E. Preedy collection]

Compound 4-4-0 No.41160, of Crewe North, at Cheadle Hulme on 5 April 1953 with a Euston train. This locomotive was the first of the batch of 40 built for the L M S R at Vulcan Foundry (from 1925 to 1927). By the date of this photograph the first withdrawals of the 'Crimson Ramblers' had begun and all had gone by 1961.

[N. E. Preedy collection]

An early spring scene in Cheshire, with 'Jubilee' No.45595 *Southern Rhodesia* crossing Holmes Chapel Viaduct, 12 April 1958. Another month or so and the trees will obscure almost all that can be seen of the brick arches. [N. E. Preedy collection]

Sir Henry Fowler's Class 7F 0-8-0 was not the best of his designs, its durability in service between shoppings being marred by inadequate coupled-wheel bearings. Nevertheless, to most lineside enthusiasts, they were handsome and photogenic machines which bespoke 'Derby' in every inch of their appearance. Loose-coupled mineral trains were their *forte* in ex-Midland and ex-L & Y areas, as with No. 49582 in this timeless scene at Chinley North Junction, 3 September 1955.
[N. E. Preedy collection]

No. 46203 *Princess Margaret Rose* passing Heaton Norris on 28 April 1956 with a Euston to Manchester express. Allocated to Edge Hill shed, she was one of the regulars on Liverpool and Manchester expresses.

[N. E. Preedy collection]

A humdrum yet nostalgic scene by Chinley North Junction box, with the signalman watching Fowler 4F No. 44030 pass on a local passenger train. Apart from their MR predecessors, these LMS 0-6-0 'all rounders' were built from 1924 to 1928 and again, surprisingly, from 1937 to 1941, coming from four of the company's workshops and four outside locomotive builders.

[N. E. Preedy collection]

'Jubilee' No. 45712 *Victory* leaving Doveholes Tunnel in the heart of the Peak District with an up St. Pancras express, 13 April 1958. The deep cutting here through massive limestone provides a setting typical of the area. The tunnel, almost two miles long, is near the summit of a climb almost unbroken for seventeen miles south from Cheadle Heath, much of it at 1 in 90. [N. E. Preedy collection]

One of the last three ex-MR Class 2F 4ft 11in 0-6-0s to remain in service, No. 58148, shunts the Leicester West Bridge branch at Glenfield on 22 November 1963. [A. R. Butcher]

An assortment of motive power on Derby shed, 7 July 1963; Horwich
Mogul No. 42846, Fowler 4F No. 44556, Stanier 8F No. 48153, B R Standard
Class 5 No. 75064 and, on the right, a B R Standard 9F.   [P. H. Wells]

Class 5 No. 44712 leaving Seaton Junction in Rutland for Market Harborough with a Great Yarmouth–Birmingham S.O. summer special in 1964. One of the later Horwich 'Black Fives' of post-war build, No. 44712, is from Rugby shed (2A), which for some years had the largest allocation of the class of any English shed.   [P. H. Wells]

The tradition of piloting on the Midland main line lasted almost to the end of steam, principally using aged Class 2P 4-4-0s to help Jubilees keep to the XL limit timings. The four LM Region express categories in order of timing were; unlimited load, limited load, special limit and XL limit—with the latter the fastest. If the load was greater than permitted for the locomotive class, the driver was entitled to a pilot and without one he was not held responsible for time lost. Here No. 45573 *Newfoundland*, leaving Luton (Midland) with a train from Leeds on 14 March 1958, is over the nine-coach XL limit and has No. 40580 as pilot.

[J. R. Besley]

The 'Crimson Ramblers' appeared in black in BR days but the pre-war nickname still remained. No. 41094, from Bedford shed, is about to depart from St. Albans with a Bedford–St. Pancras semi–fast, 22 March 1952. Once they were into their stride, these 4-4-0s were fast running but they were 'slippery' on starting, whilst the value of compounding was seldom realised in day-to-day running.   [P. J. Lynch]

Ivatt 2-6-2T No. 41289, seen at Fenny Stratford on the Bedford–Bletchley line, exemplifies the post-war trend to more functional design, without any frills, aimed at cheapness of construction and maintenance. Exposed plumbing is perhaps the most immediate feature in this scene; considerations of efficiency apart, one wonders what Sir Henry Fowler would think of this front end.

[L. Waters]

Class 4P 2-6-4T No. 42682 with an up freight passing through Luton, 22 September 1962. [A. R. Butcher]

The 6.8 p.m. Moorgate–St. Albans leaving Elstree Tunnel on 7 July 1955 behind Class 3P 2-6-2T No.40039. This was one of the twenty in the class fitted with condensing apparatus and Weir feed pumps. It has also been modified to improve performance by fitting a larger diameter Stanier chimney and blastpipe, plus outside steam pipes. [R. K. Taylor]

'Jubilee' No. 45654 *Hood*, from Sheffield (Millhouses), blows off steam at St. Pancras while waiting to leave with the 3.15 p.m. to Bradford on 12 July 1957. 'Jubilees' were the staple express motive power on the Midland main line despite its stiff gradients, supplemented by a few 'Britannias' and Rebuilt Scots—the latter being restricted in the number of platform roads they could use at St. Pancras on account of clearances. The speed limit on the Midland Division was always lower than on the Western Division and up to 1956, at a maximum of 75mph, was the lowest of any on British Railways. Thereafter it was increased to 85 mph.

[J. R. Besley]

Scenes near Barking in Essex, on 25 July 1956, on the former LT & S lines which passed from LMSR control to the jurisdiction of Eastern Region: above, Class 3F 0-6-0T No. 47512 on an up freight valiantly keeping pace with an electric, and ex-LT & S Class 3P 4-4-2T No. 41978 (below) drifting by with another local freight.

[R. K. Taylor]

Stanier's superb design of 2-8-0 for the LMS was chosen by the Government as the standard freight locomotive to be built by all the railway companies during the war years. All the major English workshops built them in quantity, including 80 at Swindon from 1943 to 1945. One of these, No.8432, drifts past Cowley Bridge Junction at Exeter with a down freight for Plymouth on 26 August 1946. The following year she was transferred to the LMS to Derby shed; as No.48432 she was withdrawn in 1966.   [Brian A. Butt]

Resplendent in the black livery which—when clean—suited the Stanier Class 5 so well, No.5025 in steam at Haworth on the Keighley & Worth Valley Railway on 3 April 1971. She was restored here prior to being moved to the Strathspey Railway in Inverness-shire. [R. H. Short]

Overleaf: another scene of preserved LMS steam, with 2-6-0 No.46443 heading out of Bewdley on an afternoon train to Bridgnorth, 22 August 1974. [J. R. Besley]